Yelping the Tegmine

poems by

Cal Freeman

Finishing Line Press
Georgetown, Kentucky

Yelping the Tegmine

ACKNOWLEDGMENTS

I'd like to thank the editors of the following journals and publications for
first featuring these poems:

Bracken Magazine: "Words for Port Austin"
Belt Magazine: "Adrian Dantley (AD) Circa 1890s" and "Yelping the Huron
    River Inn"
The Book of Donuts (Terrapin Press): "Epistle to the Donut Shop"
Cape Cod Poetry Review: "Letter From the Toledo Hollywood Casino" and
    "Poem for Geraldine"
Exacting Clam: "Echo's"
Flyover Country: "Bella Vista" and "Waltz Inn"
Ligeia Magazine: "Yelping the Tegmine" and "Text Message to My Stepson"
Oxford American: "Ode to Coca-Cola, Helium, Carbon"
Of Rust and Glass Anthology: Volume 2: "Miller's"
Open: A Journal of Arts & Letters: "Canada, Approximately" and
    "Giacometti's Heads"
Pøst: "Dichotomy Paradox as Non-Fungible Token"
Quarter After Eight: "Grammar of the Birds"
River Heron Review: "On the PFC Ronald Fitch Memorial Highway"
The William and Mary Review: "Derecho"

Publisher: Leah Huete de Maines
Editor: Christen Kincaid
Cover Art: Matt Balcer
Author Photo: Matt Balcer
Cover Design: Elizabeth Maines McCleavy

Order online: www.finishinglinepress.com
        also available on amazon.com

Author inquiries and mail orders:
Finishing Line Press
PO Box 1626
Georgetown, Kentucky 40324
USA

Contents

Dichotomy Paradox as a Non-Fungible Token

I want a different year in clean white snow.
I want the rapid senescence afforded the possum
before trauma. Just before that moment of collapse.
It's not for play. It's so it can't remember what befalls it.
A possum isn't playing possum. I want my father back.
I want a different father with the same tastes
and the same loves. I want a different flower
than what blooms in the boxwood hedges
without germination. I want to read the book
Melville's Final Voyage which my father owns in a dream.
I'm not a seafarer, but I'm not faring well,
I want to say. The snow that fell as heavy slush
early in the day has turned to eider down.
People move and of course the mounds of snow
drift and the plows drive like nobody exists.
When the streets are revealed, they're irrevocably changed,
cratered like the moon or the bottom of a sea.
A neighbor offered me her snowblower,
but I prefer shovel marks knife-edge to the driveway.
It's hard to imagine what the phrase "coming back"
must've meant once. To have it mean anything
one would have to watch the plow returning
and not have picked up the trajectory of the turn
before the vehicle began coming back.
One would have to want to have a different life
in clear white snow and want a different bloom
than the one created by the snow that February day
along the boxwood hedgerows with wine
in the decanter and thought-heavy thoughts
for the ones who left us in the garden. My voice hissing
through clenched teeth. I want a different echo
than the possum. I want a different name.
For as long as I can remember
I've been both annoyed and haunted by my name.
I don't think this is a unique relationship
to have to one's name. I imagine everyone
is at times annoyed and at other times haunted

by their names, but I dwell on mine far too much.
Others are even brave enough to change them,
and I'm not talking about some monosyllabic nom de plume
haphazardly applied, but legally change them.
My name is why it takes me so long to clear the car,
to broom it off before starting it and scraping the windows.
These are too many names and numerals for one life,
but they're so indelibly correct that I hum them
in the cold snow and again in the warm car.
It's what I don't know back there at the root
and am too listless to learn that does the haunting.
It's who I don't know. It's the theology of Jean Cauvin
and how he came to be known as John Calvin.
The prevenient grace some of them have been afforded.
I give up a little more every day. I drive to Bar 342
for corned beef sliders. I read Fanny Howe's *Second Childhood*
as I sip Canadian Club whiskey and wait for my lunch.
The man next to me has a voice like a half-empty matchbox
rattling itself awake. He doesn't know how
he's doing yet. He's here to retrieve a car
left in the parking lot. He asks if the Howe
is my AA booklet. *John John John and John* I read
in "Between Delays." I underline the four instances
of my name with a keno pencil.
John is his name too, I find out, and his voice
isn't like a matchbox I decide as I note the slack skin
around his throat, it's more like an accidental whisper,
a light breeze over dying wheat. I tell him I'd have flunked out
within a few hours, but I've got step one down
(I don't think you can actually flunk out of their program).
I read a poem called "Loneliness," scarf down my sliders,
and pay my tab. There's too much data in this place—
Keno screens, an internet jukebox, a baby shower
with a chicken wing buffet. There's too much data
in the enjambed lines of the book, what a friend of mine
has called "hangnail stanzas," for me to latch onto
anything other than my name and this personification

of loneliness that might engage such a name in actions
like clearing snow and driving to lunch.
John follows me out. A green balloon is trapped
in the door handle. He warns me not to pop it.
He paraphrases the Book of John as he lights a cigarette,
says the truth will set me free. John's my name, he explains,
and that's from the Book of John and I should try to live
my life by the idea that the truth will set you free.
I thank him. I don't tell him how homonyms ensnare us
or how the sunlight on ragged snow renders the romance
of hunkering down remote. It's too easy to drive now.
For anyone to truly come back the road would have to adopt
a chronology of hours. I don't want the road to adopt
a chronology of hours. I could be going out
for all they know. They who paved this road with too many miles.
The more of it they plow, the less of me spins out.
There's an elegance to Zeno's paradox that circumvents
the civic mind and a loveliness to leftover weather
that one mustn't lose in the sun.
I need to have my tires rotated, something. A good barroom
needs good haruspices the way prophecy needs a self to fulfill
its self-fulfilling augurs. They don't have to do much
but observe the damage and guess right.
I'll heat my liver for a reading any afternoon.

Epistle to the Donut Shop

Dear Warren Avenue, dear aluminum green awning
beneath which people waiting for the Dearborn bus
would dodge the rain: Polish women in dripping babushkas
clutching shopping bags from Fairlane Mall, young Black men
headed for the suburbs to look for work, Lebanese
millwrights going home from a grueling shift at Rouge,
dear Golden Boy Donuts, I write to you as I would write
to my parents if letters were still necessary, and they are,
of course, just as every outmoded medium gives us
so much we do not know we need. Dear father
seated in a booth behind a wall of windows drinking coffee,
reading student essays pulled from an ink-scarred manila folder,
glancing out at the avenue guttering with puddles
and discarded shopping bags while my three-year-old self eats
glazed cake donut holes and listens to Helen and Elizabeth,
immigrant first cousins who owned the place, speak to each other
in Polish (my childhood is narrated by languages
I still don't understand except in cadence and intent,
my mother speaking Spanish with Maria Chavez,
our next door neighbor, for hours while the neighborhood
kids ran in the spume of an uncapped hydrant in July;
Shahnaz Shamsedean calling her children in in Arabic
as the streetlights buzzed on). I would watch the water runnel
off of you and splay like feathers. Once I tripped in a mud puddle
in the alley, and Helen fished me out and bathed me
in the prep kitchen where they kneaded and cut the dough
and sifted powdered sugar over the Euclidian shapes of pastries,
swaddling me in warm dish towels while we waited
for my clothes to dry. My mother worked midnights in triage
at Receiving Hospital, and she would sleep during the day,
which meant that while we were eating donuts, she was dreaming
of gunshot victims and the stunned doughy faces of cardiac
arrest, of stab wounds like sequined dime purses, near overdoses
with glassy eyes and pustuled forearm scabs, police badges
glinting in halogen light, which meant that while
my father read bad prose written by the 18-year-old
children of autoworkers for Composition I at Wayne State

University, my mother's dreams were narrated by a tinny voice
reciting injuries and traumas into an analogue telephone
receiver over a crackling PA. Dear donut shop,
you are gone, not gone exactly, but your lime-green façade
has been painted pink and your smell of dough and coffee
has been replaced by garlic and kibbeh, and the family
that owns this place came here fleeing a war the way
Helen and Elizabeth came here fleeing war in a wholly
different world, yet a world defined by those twin forces
of violence and refuge, and I love this place still as I love
my mother and father while remembering donut holes
and steaming Styrofoam cups of coffee. Dear Hamido Restaurant,
dear Golden Boy, dear father, dear mother traumatized by all
that you have seen, dear Dearborn, I eat kafta in the same
building, watching the blacktop avenue blear with rain
and oil, women in hijabs pushing little wire carts out
of Arab markets, abjad liturgical script above the English
signage, and I'm nostalgic for what hasn't really changed.

Bella Vista

You're staying in Room 8. You like it here, despite the musty smell. You can watch the lake from the picnic table on the patio. "Bella Vista" is spelled out in bold cursive on the concrete bottom of the pool. It feels good to say it aloud—Bella Vista, beautiful view, grand view. It doesn't translate perfectly, but you look out and there's Lake Huron's Saginaw Bay; it's ocean-blue or blue as the sky or blue as what we maim in our descriptions. The waves this evening are whitecapped combers that spray the support bars of the jet ski lift before collapsing in a despondent clop in the sand. They haven't hosted weddings at the Bella Vista in years, but they still advertise this service on every room door. *Of all the marriages doomed to failure, why have so many of the profligate befriended me?* seems like a question for the shuttered ballroom or a prescient epithalamium. Is it something other than doom that keeps the vows coming but not keeping? A tacit understanding that ten good years beats ten lonely ones? The wisdom of knowing that forever is a concept which, despite our formal histrionics, can never be convincingly acted out? Weddings are soliloquies; marriages are more than that. A steel swing set is anchored in the breakwater. Kid Rock blares from someone's Bluetooth speaker. You want to say it doesn't sound like here, but how could it not sound like here? You're somewhere south of the Big Dipper, unsure if that makes sense. The lone maple soughs in humid air. The shouting next door's become rhapsodic. Drunks cloak themselves in noise, but it's really more akin to resignation. Too late for apology or grace. The gone years, the wasted calligraphy and crepe. You step into a swing and boomerang over the water. You think it might be Tawas across the bay. You went to a wedding there once that took place behind a little blue cottage on the banks of the Au Sable. Now they've sold the place and split the money. *Nothing really ends*, you think, looking out across the lake and knowing otherwise. Shadow of a pier in the light of a buoy that tells you you're returning to something: song, place, or figment. Superior mirage, lights, refraction, inversion of air masses revealing the impossible—a buoyant city, a levitating ship.

Echo's

The quality of the perch isn't why
a restaurant succeeds or fails, but I miss
the pan-fried perch at Echo's. Fresh Lake Erie perch,
lightly-breaded, a recipe the family would never divulge
when I asked them. I never caught their names,
but I feel awful they didn't make it.
When I was a kid, this place
was called Chaim Sweeney's and
Charlie Taylor used to sing here (there?),
and unless you heard him do
"The Wild Colonial Boy" and "The Flower
of Sweet Strabane," you likely have no affinity
for this place. Affixing new names
to buildings without structurally changing them
does a lot for ambiance though.
It gives an architecture to memories real
and imagined, personal or channeled
from the muddled anachrony of décor,
the palimpsestic layering of linoleum and wallpaper.
Chaim Sweeney was the world's foremost authority
on the hamburger, the menu said,
and I wouldn't blame anyone for thinking
this was bombast since the hamburgers
at the eponymous restaurant were unremarkable.
I'd ride in the back seat of my grandmother's Ford Escort wagon
down Outer Drive, that high curving road
commissioned by the WPA
to ribbon the perimeter of Detroit,
that uncompleted road, that floodplain
tracing the southern bend of the cantankerous Ecorse River,
to hear old Charlie sing. He'd let me sit at the edge
of the stage and strum Irish rebel songs
on my plastic guitar during his breaks.
Chaim Sweeney pissed his money
out the door on live entertainment,
which is ostensibly an enticement
to draw beer drinkers in,

but Echo's was doomed at the naming.
I think of Echo's story and a

                              caterwaul of the gone rings out
                                 drowns the preening boy
                     and lifts him off in the face of half-voiced
                                                    predation
                           he was not so special they never are
                  she chattered nonsensically during Jove's trysts
                                 to slow Juno's pursuit deleted
                                  all prefixes muted vocatives
                       the effect only approximating the sound
                              of sound returning she clutched
                                     the leaning putrefaction
                             the boy in putrefaction in tableau
                                as what she once was ossified
                         and was chiseled into a practice chanter
                           for oblivion what could be more loved
                             than what was almost lived in
                            gone marmoreal memorial *I'm yours*
                              and all the business *enjoy my body*
                            and all the unpleasant business
                       of malediction parroted with a banality
                             charming as charmed *Ah me*
                                      to repeat Ah me
                          as the business goes belly-up

I wanted to talk about the songs
of a dead folk singer who was friends
with my grandparents, a man who could
describe your sad sack story back to yourself
like Demodocus at the Mead Hall on Scherie.
I wanted to talk about perch and the imperiled
fisheries of Southeast Michigan, the restaurants
where the fishers sent their catches.
The phosphorous in the fields, blue-green algae in the harbor.
The reference to Lake Erie

I found while reading *Finnegan's Wake*
in Echo's Restaurant one January afternoon—
our lake lemanted, that greyt lack…
urban and orbal, though seep froms umber
under wasseres of Erie. The owner asked,
"Did it stop for a merciful moment, the ice storm?"
It had me thinking of the adjective "merciful"
because I'm also scared
all the time of death and money,
of paucity and grift, by what might arrive in the mail
with the clap of tin, by excessive bilirubin
in the blood (can't be a liver and have a liver,
the ale taster in the night book says).
I'd watch the Lions at Echo's every Sunday
while reading a book and eating perch,
which sounds a lot like losing in Loserville
but the Lions have a way of getting you to pay
attention, which is to say they have unique
ways of losing, ways you haven't yet imagined.
They slow the awful sabbath down.
There's rarely such a chance to gaze languorously
inward and taste the afternoon like a morsel
(egg, flour, lemon, tartar sauce, the flesh of freshwater).

Yelping the Tegmine

It is a cluster in the constellation Cancer
and a crab shack near the Shell station on Telegraph Road.
The polysemy and the crab salad sandwiches are delicious.

The trains in these parts can hobble your commute,
and if your inclination
is not to trust crab salad from a shot-and-beer roadhouse,
even a well-reviewed one, I don't blame you.

I recommend the sandwich though. It's flavorful and fresh,
and the area won't suffer for having hosted you.

They'll never buy into your epiphanies, so don't pretend to have them.
The moon is not a skiff with your inky spleen in its paren,
and the nearby park is not a closed paren within which
you might make a notation about Tycho Brahe's bare-eyed observations.

There is a sadness to bisque and beer, which is why I'm suggesting
the crab sandwich, the Zeta Cancri signature sandwich.

They'll never ask you to Yelp the place either. An old trucker friend
of mine lived upstairs after a bad break-up with his ex.

It's not much of a story: scotography, x-ray radiography,
a couple of boys were whooping it up, writing out the darkness.
The false ceiling, the dim lights, the wickerwork like bones.

It's a new year. It's the ecliptic of oil tankers
in the eyeline of that long glacial plain.
You must keep the big rigs' occultation in mind and search
unbidden Yelp reviews.
The afternoon's less dull for the thoughts of stars.

You don't have to sit here while you eat.
You can take the sandwich to the park and hiss back at the geese,
or do the geese honk? I believe it's both, and they also shit like dogs,
so maybe it's best to dine in and ask for a boilermaker.

Listen for whatever beered-up nonsense echoes down the pine
and know there's a pleasant way of disappearing
in such a place without feeling quite alone.
If you sit upright in the stool, you can watch the bubbles

decamp for foam. It's a bird's-eye, not a god's-eye view
from above the ecliptic line the room can get on you.
The crab is not endemic to this place; it isn't what you'd call
"To die for," but as I've said elsewhere, it's very good.

Grammar of the Birds

It's the late offseason of what
will never be. The RV park
by the inland sea is empty.
I clamber onto the exposed
poplar roots, their earth
gone to wind and surf,
to listen. A grist of calcium
sparkles in the sand.
The cooling towers
of the Fermi I and II reactors
exhale little puffs of steam
into the netted-mackerel sky
across the bay.
I've been hearing it since
before the dawn,
this finite automaton
syntax of the birds.
I've been a blind jag
between the branches,
a bigram in a phonological
bout, a memory house
made ridiculous
by repetition. These
two-birds-in-the-hand
truisms, this robin trill.
Without plumage,
I've been a hopeless birder
of disembodied song.
The Huron River Inn
at the mouth of the bay
is closed. There's a fishing boat
at the edge of the gravel lot,
some steelhead skeletons
combed over by the gulls.
Which is to say we become
what we cannot look
forward to, the way

a gastropod coils around
itself what is and is not
itself only to be plucked
through its aperture like light.

Yelping a Bar Louie

I'll have to say goodbye to this vale
of daytime drunks someday,
but for now I'm meeting Jason Storms at 1:15
to talk about Book XI of Milton's epic. He says
we blame ourselves whether or not we have
selves to blame—a mangled car in a copse
of trees, almost daily self-flagellations
with the barely quaffable. Storms,
not Milton, says this, but to say it
he draws from a couple of Milton's
favorite themes: the tragedy of predestination,
self-doom. Synods are for angels.
Can't get more than a couple of us
in one place, even a weekly meet-up
can *in substance feel grievous to bear.*
I'm pretty sure it's some kind of ruse,
you're thinking; there's nobody named Storms
sight-reading devotional hymns
and scanning lines of blank verse.
But there are so many implausible stories
that end up being true. We know, for instance,
what we know of death because a serpent spoke
into our mother's ear to teach that God
attributes to place no sanctity. Bar Louie
(there are 73 of them nationwide)
is *sad, noisome, dark,* but the mind mythologizes
fact to make it feel less alone. They don't toggle
the liquor from those digital stoppers;
as a result, the concoctions actually do their work.
It's easy to be here, puzzling over
Noah's raven, wondering what dry land
it may've found amidst the deluge.

Derecho

What does it mean that you lived on Shenandoah Street,
a name so far removed from its whistling valley?

Near the back of the yard was a concrete slab stained
tobacco brown by eastern cottonwood leaves.

Those trees grow too quick, top-heavy and weak
in sandy loam, routinely toppling in summer storms.

Once there was a shed there, but it was blown away
by the green storm of 1980. The trace is a great container

for the aorist tense. It's a serrated, toothy leaf.
It's a great leaf shape for tracing and incising what's befallen

me and has befallen you before and thus keeps. Even the tree
is gone, I meant to say. The tree is unsurprisingly gone,

I meant to say. My father saw a Volkswagon fall
from the sky into the parking lot of Amado's Restaurant

on his way home. He and my mother huddled in the stairwell
where there were no windows. I love what it means

for trees felled by storms before your birth to cradle
concrete in their roots. I love the way the bowed

fence post can't go back to how it was but tells us
how it was all the same. You can get forty years

out of a good fence post. I've gotten close to that
out of comparable equipment. I meant to say I'm afraid

of storms and other things as I stagger into middle age.
I meant to find a more precise noun than things, Shenandoah,

whistling valley. I meant to say you can't see the middle
from where you're at, to explain my use of second person

sooner, how its reverse bow echo is meant to foretell
a straight-line wind. How I meant to say has less to do

with botched intentions than the mystery of utterance itself.
How I hope we don't become what we haven't said.

Adrian Dantley (AD) Circa 1890s

The night Larry Bird famously stole Isiah Thomas' inbound pass
I was with my mother at Circa 1890s Saloon
across Cass Avenue from Wayne State University
where my father was teaching *The Tempest*
to a group of bored undergrads in State Hall.
It was 1987, or circa 1890 if one takes the long view of history.
Adrian Dantley (AD) was my favorite Pistons player that year.
My mother was bantering with a drunk Boston fan
who, as she put it, "was looking to get his teeth knocked out
rooting for Boston in a Cass Corridor bar."
My father let his class out early to catch the end of the game.
We had them down one with three seconds to go
and possession of the ball. It looked like
we were coming back to Detroit with a 3-2 series lead
and were finally going to vanquish the Celtics.
"Larry Bird sucks eggs on Saturday nights,"
my mother taunted the guy. It was Tuesday.
My parents shared an '85 Ford Escort back then,
and we picked my father up from work
Tuesday nights so he didn't have to ride
the Warren Avenue bus after dark.
My father laughed at my mother's trash talking
as he sipped his Newcastle Ale. Gone now
circa 2020 is Circa 1890s, its façade of curved
white pillars that never blocked the rain
and faded to the color of cigarette ash
as the paint leached and decades passed,
known as "the teeth" to Wayne State students, gone.
All bars circa 1890s get loud with animated talk
about little matters that matter little alone
but creep up in aggregate at the end of a stanza.
Basketball is a series of meticulous little matters.
AD and Bill Laimbeer setting brutal, off-the-ball
screens out of bounds. Barroom histrionics
around cathode-ray tube televisions, full fathom five
into which the ghost of Boston Garden stowed
our hopes (in the deciding game seven AD

would knock himself unconscious diving
for a loose ball). Wondrous and strange,
my mother's invective, the beer foam in my father's beard,
Larry Bird stepping before that fated pass
like an interference beam (the holomovement
that holds them there in their spectral dimensions),
his quick toss to Dennis Johnson for a layup
with a second left. AD dropped 25 in game five.
His right leg was two inches shorter than his left,
but he had a such a quick first step (Kevin McHale
was a wicket jammed in wet cement
when he tried to guard him) and a deadly flat-footed shot.
Isiah never liked him, though, and Dennis Rodman
got too many minutes for his taste. When they traded AD in 1989,
I sobbed on my mother's shoulder in our living room
(yellow light on rough-hewn mahogany paneling,
all that never happens in the interior of a place
happens to us, directly, there. The secret
mind of a university swimming in imported tap beer
and popcorn, free popcorn. Circa 1890s,
a joke that was easy to miss but would define
an epoch in a public university's life)
like we were saying goodbye forever to somebody
we loved. It's the first time I remember feeling that way.

Waltz Inn

A heavy oak door
has opened of its own volition
after having just been closed,
and the figure of a woman
looks at our troubled time
in languor. A spirited restaurant
where each denizen believes
in spirits. I'd have liked
to have gone back one more time
for unwooded chardonnay
and lightly-pankoed perch,
to swallow spirits and ghost,
to take something for the ditch,
but all I have is the old farmhouse
in my viewfinder and another plaintive
photo for a relic. 19th-century
farmhouse storied of good food
and visitations. Maple bar
with backlit mirrors rimed,
soon to be gone as the gone trees
of Whispering Woods,
gone as the figures the night cuts
of parallax and artificial light.
If I listen I can almost hear
the clip-clop of hooves
in the fresh hell of half-sleep,
the clatter of iron and steel tolling over
hash marks as an engine tumbles
toward the city. Such repetition
is how every ghost is born.
In the headlight of a train,
the atemporal's a fact,
the known's a whistle stop,
the mind a token visitation.

Words for Port Austin

The waxing crescent moon's an open paren where any anecdote might fit.
You think you're thinking but those mechanisms are gummed like the orb
    weaver's ticks.
This cloying sense of the real we measure every experience against—the
    bluebird and the swan
in the back dune swale do not seem real.
I get an email from the writer RS Deeren. He grew up in Caro, Michigan
and said he never really saw anyone else writing about Michigan's Thumb
    but told me he had swum
in the Pinnebog River and eaten ice cream in Grindstone as a boy.
I tell him I hiked the trail behind The Buccaneer Den this morning. Its
    dusty windows
are peppered with "No Parking" and "No Trespassing" signs.
One of the few extant Yelp reviews of the place comes from Jennie S
and reads, "The elderly workers were rude and did not want us there.
They actually made us get our own menu off someone's table (yes, while
    they were eating).
The elderly bartender spilled my drink, bringing it to me half-full.
I was sitting at the bar, not a table. Didn't offer to refill it. I asked several
    other questions
about Port Austin and apparently I was bothering them."
This used to be a supper club, and in the afternoon anglers would bring
    their catches
to sell or have them cleaned and fried on site.
The pin oaks have ampersands for leaves and roots that go on and on in
    polysyndeton.
The benefit of boarded-up rural supper clubs with scabbed-up motel
pools abutting state lands stitched with hiking trails leading to scenic
vistas above lakes is that even those
who were never in the business of marram grass can imagine the
    succession
of small ecosystems culminating in the ominous shadows of scrub oak.
This afternoon I watched a tractor uproot jet ski lifts from shallow water.
It marked the end of a season that never really was.
I snap a picture on my phone and caption it, *You can't see the lights*
of Standish from a beachhead in Port Austin because there are no lights
in Standish. It only becomes a beachhead

if we think of dusk as a militaristic advance. Crows at the shoreline,
	or maybe grackles,
a swan so white and hyperreal against the blue it looks ornamental.
I refuse to say the swan's a trumpeter; it sounds political, and, like
	you, I'm dealing with
a plurality of morons who look for blazons of sun on water, which I
also do, who comment on the breadth of the beach this year, which I
also do. The water is low, and we have ten extra feet of sand. I won't
say, *All littorals are false*, for fear of where the metaphor might go.
The beach is an obscene place, and no obscenity can be construed as
	false.
The glistening breadth of sand, the high-water scum of last year's
	flotsam before the seawall,
a man blowing hopelessly into a pair of water wings (once I realized
nothing had ever been innocent I kept on writing about what had yet
to happen to the self in a notational,
atemporal parenthetical I hadn't planned on including). I won't say I
	have heroes,
but if I did, they would be writing *Sleepless Nights* and quoting
	Aeschylus.
Somebody should buy the Buccaneer and rehab it, fix up the motel,
bring up singers from Detroit every weekend like they used to.
I watch a girl take a large plastic shovel to a mound of sand and shape
	it
into the likeness of a castle. Moon in a daytime sky, stand of paper
	birches
on a tombolo bayed at by the bay, a reflection the tideless weight of
here won't close.

Letter From the Toledo Hollywood Casino

Dear Vester, I write to you in open-G
in hopes the train that you were waiting for
is gone, along with the blood harmonies
and demotic outfits, those mesh trucker hats
and denim overalls. Your catgut scuffle, the trite
steam whistle, that damned snare pulled taut
with treble strings, I haven't quite caught up to
the times either, Vester. I drove past Custer's
obsidian statue in Monroe, Michigan yesterday.
He was scrabbling down a stallion's flank
with a buck knife in his teeth, alive enough
to listen to the 18-wheelers on the interstate.
You see, it's hard to get nostalgic for cavalry
or trains. This is the epoch of the big rig,
not the banjo. I write from an interior that isn't
real. You're acquainted with the bespectacled
dog on the drink coaster at the Johnny Vegas Café,
aren't you, Vester? It puts me in mind
of you, somehow. A giant PVC pipe pours
rainwater from the roof into The Maumee River
Valley where chucked tires suck phosphorous
and mud. Last night the orbs of floating lanterns
lit the sky above the bridge like a string of Jupiters.
Today, loons ingest the skeins and sick up
in the flats. From this windowless place
beyond reverence where the nickel slot machines
clang and blink in a nimbus of cigarette smoke,
I'll cast again into the fatalistic waters.
I'm not high anymore, Vester, it's just
that the walleye have minted my irises
on a bed of sediment and turned them into silver
coins in the tumble of a wish, taunting,
You must remember this: it's a certain kind
of singing about a certain kind of nothing that sticks.

On the PFC Ronald Fitch Memorial Highway

I think about the malfunctioning
M-16s of the Vietnam War
and how some weapons
use their children as mothers.
I try to remember the eponymous
PFC—that's a leg
of Highway 127 for anyone
who prefers numerical logic.
I go with proper nouns into
Bellingar Specialty Meats
and come out with two venison
cutlets and some jerky.
I'm not saying you should
suspend your politics
or be interpellated by the miles,
I'm saying that you will.
I'd describe the maize fields
as ribboning,
and I haven't even seen them
at twilight. You can't talk sense
into the mergansers
and Canada geese that sup
blue-green algae in the millpond
(and I'm told there are such people)
or the tragedians of Fitch's war.
The silos of the granary slacken
their attention on these sunlit days.
I work jerky in yellow teeth.
You were south of 20, Fitch,
nearing a birthday. The name
comes home to ribbon (the name
a homing device, the worm
your emperor of Lineland)
a stretch of asphalt like a white line.

Poem for Geraldine

With all of Palm Beach singing Jimmy Buffet songs,
I tried to dig a piece of pulled pork from between
my teeth with a toothpick shaped like a patio umbrella.
The purple hummingbird planted in the brick-red mulch
wafted its wings, plastic jobs affixed to the torso
by tiny springs that approximate a live flutter
in the breeze. The bird had to be bigger than the real
bird to be ornamental, to be seen, but the bird wasn't unreal,
it was a gift from Geraldine who died three years ago.
I wonder if a Palm Beach wind in plastic wings
means that her spirit is nearby. Yes, it's Geraldine,
she's wearing a Hawaiian shirt and a loud sun visor
with parrots on the bill. She's drinking a piña colada
with one of these crepe umbrellas jammed in the shaved ice,
a long Maverick menthol dangling from her lip.
I'm still looking for her when the gulf breeze
soughs the fronds, when they belt out "Nautical Wheelers"
and a few of them stagger on the nude cement
in the bald sun, sweet leathered skin, sweet rum,
sweet cabana cream, sweet flesh on a bed of open coals.

Giacometti's Heads

In Café du Dôme the waiter's head
was tumescent and hyperreal,
the street beyond
the plate glass window
a spindled shadow perched
on a sloping bank.
Not that metonym for mind,
but the globe of bone
it's physiologically impossible
to carry. What he saw:
vegetal skulls screwed
on jagged lines distending
toward the void.
He sculpted the body from bodies
of decomposing plaster,
each new piece a crumbling
maquette of itself.
The heads were chiseled
antonyms of heart,
his muses demimondes
he berated and destroyed.
Most art isn't art but decoration,
he told Pablo Picasso.
Hands Holding the Void,
breasts thrust before
the guillotine, feet like claws
scrabbling their roost.
The Chariot with no phaeton,
shambolic lines astride a steeple box,
ponderous skull on shoulders
that would fall flat
as a squashed roach
in any other world.
As he watched his own
shadow leash to him
and lead him down
the boulevard

after exiting the cinema
on Montparnasse, he asked
his mute walking companion
Samuel Beckett, *In what heart*
does maundering
turn to cataclysm? That's
the desiccated figure
I would make.
Neither thought epiphany
could save them
nor believed musculature
could make us real.

Ode to Coca-Cola, Helium, Carbon

A half-drunk bottle of Coca-Cola
rests on Johnny McGlynn's tombstone.
A couple of helium balloons are tied to it too.
Sarah wonders what the story is.
Neither of us knew Johnny McGlynn,
brand-loyal McGlynn, lover of soda pop
McGlynn. He's neighbors
with my father now. My father's his new neighbor.
Sarah left wire flowers in the brass stand
next to my father's name on the black
columbarium wall across the little road
from McGlynn's tombstone.
My mother, Peggy O'Neill, picked this spot
called "companionship grove,"
for its proximity to the river.
Johnny McGlynn's Coca-Cola bottle
puts me in mind of that famous jar
in Tennessee, the way it bends
the Huron River and Huron River
Drive to the cemetery's will.
Hot Coca-Cola is disgusting
to consider on this muggy day.
It's supposed to storm later.
My mother worries about the flowers
in the rain and wind. I recite
"The Beautiful American Word,
Sure" by Delmore Schwartz
to the black marble box, but the town
of Flat Rock is stone-deaf to poetry.
You can't get the words to make music.
I'm not finishing poems much these days.
I keep name-checking my father's
favorite poets, though, instead
of saying what I don't know how to say
about finitude and grief. Death is heavy
like the tombstone of Johnny McGlynn.

It bends the space around it to accelerate
the light, but grief is more
like the helium balloons that pretend
to lift his grave; they work at it all day,
this futile lifting.
Sarah notes how strange it is to see
my mother's name beneath my father's
even though her death date's unfulfilled—
open paren, closed paren, open paren,
parents, parent. There's so much
I don't want to tell you. There's even more
I don't want to hear myself say, like
I'm equal to the task of leaving
crass symbols with the dead.
The story of Coca-Cola is well-known
and engaging for cocaine's
appearance as a character, but it's nothing
when contrasted with the story of helium,
that yellow spectral line observed
during a solar eclipse in 1868,
first among the earthly noble gases,
second among elements in ubiquity.
Carbon, which mycelium borrows
from tree roots to break down matter,
is fourth in abundance; the carbon cycle's
why there's little left of your neighbor,
Johnny McGlynn, Father.
But they treated you to fire
and put you in a box which I placed
inside the columbarium wall.
I think you'd like hearing *they treated you to fire*
from inside your marble; it reminds me
of Milton's *burning marl.*
I look at the carbonated beverage
flat in Flat Rock and remember how
I placed a box in a vault
and it made phosphorous run to the river,

and algae stopped the running river, Father.
You watch now like a heron from your
gabbled roost. Johnny McGlynn
sucks ice in 4/4 time. My mother
thinks you deserve a swifter river.
This one's gold-green like a pile
of newly minted bills or St. Patrick's Day
swag scattered in a parking lot.
Pretend luck starved of oxygen,
the way we speak of graves
and what you would've liked.

Yelping the Huron River Inn

A wreath can be good if you're walking north
or if you simply spot it on a neighbor's door
across the road. Headlights can also be good
for a mind perpetually flowing south.
I don't try to overdo it, that stuff that stultifies the tongue.
It's fearful boredom; they've left me alone with
asphalt and concrete unspooling.
I've never ended up anywhere better after driving,
but still I drive. Another wreath, this time on a transept,
this time wired to a soffit.
I've heard the mourning doves
that once populated it. People in these parts
are quick to tell you not to follow
Huron River Road past where the river bends
lest you land in Rockwood.
There's a real night out there and a cold sky
whose celestial bodies glint.
A mill pond beleaguered by the moon in water,
a jack pine stand behind a Taco Bell,
brown scrub oaks along the highway.
I've been in this business a long time,
long enough to know the price of a wreath
full of replica tanagers from the free whiskey shot
they give when the cargo train crosses the bridge
outside the window of the Huron River Inn
where twin spruces tower before
the knotty pine door, iron boar's nose
for a knocker, needles on the sidewalk
plashing beneath your shoes.

Miller's

Honor system, no bill left at your table. Cash only. Summarize what you had to the one who already knows when you are done. Plain burger medium, no cheese, two drafts, two whiskeys. Quick math and a total. I made it sound snappy when I had the energy. I'd repeat it in my head several times before I spoke. Plain burger medium no cheese two drafts two whiskeys.

Our snow day bar. Sleighs and horses and country inns and snowmen painted on the back mirror that winter night we stopped in to have burgers and Canadian Club and play a few games of euchre at a table in the corner. We could not see out, but we could sense it falling. To see is to sense, so maybe we didn't sense it, but we knew it was falling. Out there where we had just been with beards of slush in our knit hats.

When we left to walk home, the side door was stuck against a drift. I shouldered it like a sleigh and fell into the night. Behind the UPS store across the road, Molly found a hand truck a worker had forgotten to put away and proceeded to give Sarah and Emily rides between the staggered, windblown peaks of drifts. It gets beautiful and burdensome as it accumulates. We were warm from the food and whiskey, insulated from the wind and falling snow fine as eiderdown and heavy as a wet wool coat and we were ponderous as eider ducks walking through it. Molly left the hand truck where she found it. I'm sure there's some muddled footage of them cutting ruts in the alleyway and laughing.

The afternoons I spent there by myself were darker than that night. Same order. Getting right. Fanny Howe's poems on the bar top next to my beer, a High Life draft with CC back. The same, always, burdensome and beautiful as you fall. Yet it wasn't the kind of place they'd shout your name or pretend to remember you. A High Life draft with CC back, plain burger no cheese with raw onion and pickle—you can feel human again if you repeat that order. High Life draft, CC back, plain burger, no cheese, raw onion and pickle. The Canadian Club would come in a big slug in a water glass, and they'd set the burger before you on a wax paper sheet.

Text Message to My Stepson

You remember that tree of heaven,
also called stinking sumac, also called varnish

tree, also called ailanthus altissima
of the Simaroubaceae family that bowed

the fence on Drew's side
when you were a kid?

It seems serendipitous and strange
that you spent countless hours

kicking a soccer ball beneath it
and are now studying the benefits

of the quassinoids such putrefying
plant matter becomes.

What heals heals. The chain link
bellied out, the boy

you were gone to another state.

Canada, Approximately

Uncle Viktor owned a bar in Rockwood called the Tegmine after a crab-shaped group of stars in the constellation Cancer, but there's far less to steer by if you're headed toward Ontario or Monroe in a speedboat, sailboat, or cabin cruiser. I told Uncle Viktor, *If you're heading toward Put-In-Bay in your cabin cruiser, you can't be counting on the stars; you should have more than stars to go on.* I made a joke about the crab salad sandwich, his signature Zeta Cancri, and Rockwood bologna when I sat in the Tegmine one afternoon and drank. *I'll give you the river,* I said, as if it were mine, but Uncle Viktor knew the river like he knew the swollen veins on the backs of his hands. The Huron full of PFAS, gobies, and damsel flies rippling the blue-green algae. Uncle Viktor would stop his bicycle to eat a crab salad sandwich and watch the freighters plod toward the smaller islands of Ontario. Perhaps it wasn't worth it to keep the beer in the cooler and the heat in the ducts and the former owner's ghost upstairs, or to keep the taciturn old man who set out our cold longnecks in his employ behind the plank all those decades. The Tegmine won't be there when we re-emerge. The Boblo Island Amusement Park where Uncle Viktor would drive us in those emphysemic knock-off Model Ts has been gone for decades too. *Believe me when I tell you the boundary waters belie all consequence,* he said once. *I have a friend a few short nautical miles from here who remembers me as a bight before a copse of trees obscuring riverbanks through the lenses of a pair of Nikon Aculons. We don't see more precisely with binoculars or any of the Tuscan's instruments; we don't know our noses from a nation or a bar rail from a floe of river ice,* he added. It's the kind of vestigial talk that keeps a gone place alive while the bills and notices pile up. They could take the Tegmine, but he knows that group of stars like he knows his breadth of boundary waters, like he knows who hauls on waders to go haunting in our debts.

Cal Freeman was born and raised in Detroit. He is the author of the books *Fight Songs* (Eyewear 2017) and *Poolside at the Dearborn Inn* (R&R Press 2022). His writing has appeared in many journals including *Image, The Poetry Review, Verse Daily, Berfrois, The Moth, Oxford American, River Styx,* and *Hippocampus.* His poems have been anthologized in *The Poet's Quest for God* (Eyewear 2016), *Respect: the Poetry of Detroit Music* (Michigan State University Press 2020), *I Wanna Be Loved By You: Poems On Marilyn Monroe* (Milk & Cake Press 2021), *What Things Cost: An Anthology for the People* (University Press Kentucky 2022), and *Beyond the Frame* (Diode Editions 2023). He is a recipient of the Devine Poetry Fellowship (judged by Terrance Hayes), winner of *Passages North*'s Neutrino Prize, and a finalist for the *River Styx* International Poetry Prize. He teaches at Oakland University and serves as Writer-In-Residence with InsideOut Literary Arts Detroit.